ROUNDELAYS

ROUNDELAYS

Richard Kostelanetz

The New York Quarterly Foundation, Inc.
New York, New York

NYQ Books™ is an imprint of The New York Quarterly Foundation, Inc.

The New York Quarterly Foundation, Inc.
P.O. Box 2015
Old Chelsea Station
New York, NY 101113

www.nyq.org

Copyright © 2016 Richard Kostelanetz

All rights reserved. No part of this book may be used or reproduced in any matter whatsoever without written permission of the author except in the case of brief quotations embodied in critical articles and reviews.

First Edition.

Layout and Design by Andrew Charles Morinelli

Author Photo by Nona Eleanor Ellis

Library of Congress Control Number: 2016916468

ISBN: 978-1-63045-042-7

In memory of Dom Sylvester Houédard (1927-1992), who introduced me to "concrete poetry" in London fifty years later.

ARTARTART
TARTARTAR
ARTARTART
TARTARTAR
ARTARTART
TARTARTAR
ARTARTART
TARTARTAR
ARTARTART
TARTARTAR
ARTARTART
TARTARTAR
ARTARTART
TARTARTAR
ARTARTART
TARTARTAR
ARTARTART
TARTARTAR
ARTARTART
TARTARTAR

ASHASHASH
HASHASHAS
ASHASHASH
HASHASHAS
ASHASHASH
HASHASHAS
ASHASHASH
HASHASHAS
ASHASHASH
HASHASHAS
ASHASHASH
HASHASHAS
ASHASHASH
HASHASHAS
ASHASHASH
HASHASHAS
ASHASHASH
HASHASHAS

EROSEROSEROS
ROSEROSEROSE
EROSEROSEROS
ROSEROSEROSE
EROSEROSEROS
ROSEROSEROSE
EROSEROSEROS
ROSEROSEROSE
EROSEROSEROS
ROSEROSEROSE
EROSEROSEROS
ROSEROSEROSE
EROSEROSEROS
ROSEROSEROSE
EROSEROSEROS
ROSEROSEROSE
EROSEROSEROS
ROSEROSEROSE
EROSEROSEROS
ROSEROSEROSE

ENTRAPENTRAP
TRAPENTRAPEN
RAPENTRAPENT
ENTRAPENTRAP
TRAPENTRAPEN
RAPENTRAPENT
ENTRAPENTRAP
TRAPENTRAPEN
RAPENTRAPENT
ENTRAPENTRAP
TRAPENTRAPEN
RAPENTRAPENT
ENTRAPENTRAP
TRAPENTRAPEN
RAPENTRAPENT
ENTRAPENTRAP
TRAPENTRAPEN
RAPENTRAPENT
ENTRAPENTRAP
TRAPENTRAPEN
RAPENTRAPENT

FLEAFLEAFLEA
LEAFLEAFLEAF
FLEAFLEAFLEA
LEAFLEAFLEAF
FLEAFLEAFLEA
LEAFLEAFLEAF
FLEAFLEAFLEA
LEAFLEAFLEAF
FLEAFLEAFLEA
LEAFLEAFLEAF
FLEAFLEAFLEA
LEAFLEAFLEAF
FLEAFLEAFLEA
LEAFLEAFLEAF
FLEAFLEAFLEA
LEAFLEAFLEAF
FLEAFLEAFLEA
LEAFLEAFLEAF

AGITAGITAGITAGIT
TAGITAGITAGITAGI
AGITAGITAGITAGIT
TAGITAGITAGITAGI
AGITAGITAGITAGIT
TAGITAGITAGITAGI
AGITAGITAGITAGIT
TAGITAGITAGITAGI
AGITAGITAGITAGIT
TAGITAGITAGITAGI
AGITAGITAGITAGIT
TAGITAGITAGITAGI
AGITAGITAGITAGIT
TAGITAGITAGITAGI
AGITAGITAGITAGIT
TAGITAGITAGITAGI
AGITAGITAGITAGIT
TAGITAGITAGITAGI
AGITAGITAGITAGIT
TAGITAGITAGITAGI

EVILEVILEVIL
VILEVILEVILE
EVILEVILEVIL
VILEVILEVILE
EVILEVILEVIL
VILEVILEVILE
EVILEVILEVIL
VILEVILEVILE
EVILEVILEVIL
VILEVILEVILE
EVILEVILEVIL
VILEVILEVILE
EVILEVILEVIL
VILEVILEVILE
EVILEVILEVIL
VILEVILEVILE
EVILEVILEVIL
VILEVILEVILE
EVILEVILEVIL
VILEVILEVILE

INASMUCH
ASMUCHIN
MUCHINAS
CHINASMU
INASMUCH
ASMUCHIN
MUCHINAS
CHINASMU
INASMUCH
ASMUCHIN
MUCHINAS
CHINASMU
INASMUCH
ASMUCHIN
MUCHINAS
CHINASMU
INASMUCH
ASMUCHIN
MUCHINAS
CHINASMU
INASMUCH
ASMUCHIN
MUCHINAS
CHINASMU

AILMENT
MENTAIL
ENTAILM
AILMENT
MENTAIL
ENTAILM
AILMENT
MENTAIL
ENTAILM
AILMENT
MENTAIL
ENTAILM
AILMENT
MENTAIL
ENTAILM
AILMENT
MENTAIL
ENTAILM
AILMENT
MENTAIL

```
GRINGRINGRIN
RINGRINGRING
GRINGRINGRIN
RINGRINGRING
GRINGRINGRIN
RINGRINGRING
GRINGRINGRIN
RINGRINGRING
GRINGRINGRIN
RINGRINGRING
GRINGRINGRIN
RINGRINGRING
GRINGRINGRIN
RINGRINGRING
GRINGRINGRIN
RINGRINGRING
GRINGRINGRIN
RINGRINGRING
GRINGRINGRIN
RINGRINGRING
GRINGRINGRIN
RINGRINGRING
```

NAMENAMENAME
AMENAMENAMEN
NAMENAMENAME
AMENAMENAMEN
NAMENAMENAME
AMENAMENAMEN
NAMENAMENAME
AMENAMENAMEN
NAMENAMENAME
AMENAMENAMEN
NAMENAMENAME
AMENAMENAMEN
NAMENAMENAME
AMENAMENAMEN
NAMENAMENAME
AMENAMENAMEN
NAMENAMENAME
AMENAMENAMEN
NAMENAMENAME
AMENAMENAMEN

APTAPTAPTAPT
TAPTAPTAPTAP
APTAPTAPTAPT
TAPTAPTAPTAP
APTAPTAPTAPT
TAPTAPTAPTAP
APTAPTAPTAPT
TAPTAPTAPTAP
APTAPTAPTAPT
TAPTAPTAPTAP
APTAPTAPTAPT
TAPTAPTAPTAP
APTAPTAPTAPT
TAPTAPTAPTAP
APTAPTAPTAPT
TAPTAPTAPTAP
APTAPTAPTAPT
TAPTAPTAPTAP
APTAPTAPTAPT
TAPTAPTAPTAP
APTAPTAPTAPT
TAPTAPTAPTAP

HESITANT
SITANTHE
TANTHESI
ANTHESIT
THESITAN
HESITANT
SITANTHE
TANTHESI
ANTHESIT
THESITAN
HESITANT
SITANTHE
TANTHESI
ANTHESIT
THESITAN
HESITANT
SITANTHE
TANTHESI
ANTHESIT
THESITAN

```
ATEATEATEATE
TEATEATEATEA
EATEATEATEAT
ATEATEATEATE
TEATEATEATEA
EATEATEATEAT
ATEATEATEATE
TEATEATEATEA
EATEATEATEAT
ATEATEATEATE
TEATEATEATEA
EATEATEATEAT
ATEATEATEATE
TEATEATEATEA
EATEATEATEAT
ATEATEATEATE
TEATEATEATEA
EATEATEATEAT
ATEATEATEATE
TEATEATEATEA
EATEATEATEAT
```

SHRUGSHRUG
RUGSHRUGSH
SHRUGSHRUG
RUGSHRUGSH
SHRUGSHRUG
RUGSHRUGSH
SHRUGSHRUG
RUGSHRUGSH
SHRUGSHRUG
RUGSHRUGSH
SHRUGSHRUG
RUGSHRUGSH
SHRUGSHRUG
RUGSHRUGSH
SHRUGSHRUG
RUGSHRUGSH
SHRUGSHRUG
RUGSHRUGSH

USERUSERUSER
RUSERUSERUSE
USERUSERUSER
RUSERUSERUSE
USERUSERUSER
RUSERUSERUSE
USERUSERUSER
RUSERUSERUSE
USERUSERUSER
RUSERUSERUSE
USERUSERUSER
RUSERUSERUSE
USERUSERUSER
RUSERUSERUSE
USERUSERUSER
RUSERUSERUSE
USERUSERUSER
RUSERUSERUSE
USERUSERUSER
RUSERUSERUSE
USERUSERUSER
RUSERUSERUSE

ARCARCARC
CARCARCAR
ARCARCARC
CARCARCAR
ARCARCARC
CARCARCAR
ARCARCARC
CARCARCAR
ARCARCARC
CARCARCAR
ARCARCARC
CARCARCAR
ARCARCARC
CARCARCAR
ARCARCARC
CARCARCAR
ARCARCARC
CARCARCAR

APEAPEAPEAPE
PEAPEAPEAPEA
APEAPEAPEAPE
PEAPEAPEAPEA
APEAPEAPEAPE
PEAPEAPEAPEA
APEAPEAPEAPE
PEAPEAPEAPEA
APEAPEAPEAPE
PEAPEAPEAPEA
APEAPEAPEAPE
PEAPEAPEAPEA
APEAPEAPEAPE
PEAPEAPEAPEA
APEAPEAPEAPE
PEAPEAPEAPEA
APEAPEAPEAPE
PEAPEAPEAPEA
APEAPEAPEAPE
PEAPEAPEAPEA

CHINCHINCHIN
INCHINCHINCH
CHINCHINCHIN
INCHINCHINCH
CHINCHINCHIN
INCHINCHINCH
CHINCHINCHIN
INCHINCHINCH
CHINCHINCHIN
INCHINCHINCH
CHINCHINCHIN
INCHINCHINCH
CHINCHINCHIN
INCHINCHINCH
CHINCHINCHIN
INCHINCHINCH
CHINCHINCHIN
INCHINCHINCH

CODECODECODE
DECODECODECO
CODECODECODE
DECODECODECO
CODECODECODE
DECODECODECO
CODECODECODE
DECODECODECO
CODECODECODE
DECODECODECO
CODECODECODE
DECODECODECO
CODECODECODE
DECODECODECO
CODECODECODE
DECODECODECO
CODECODECODE
DECODECODECO
CODECODECODE
DECODECODECO

AVERAVERAVER
RAVERAVERAVE
AVERAVERAVER
RAVERAVERAVE
AVERAVERAVER
RAVERAVERAVE
AVERAVERAVER
RAVERAVERAVE
AVERAVERAVER
RAVERAVERAVE
AVERAVERAVER
RAVERAVERAVE
AVERAVERAVER
RAVERAVERAVE
AVERAVERAVER
RAVERAVERAVE
AVERAVERAVER
RAVERAVERAVE

DATADATADATA
TADATADATADA
DATADATADATA
TADATADATADA
DATADATADATA
TADATADATADA
DATADATADATA
TADATADATADA
DATADATADATA
TADATADATADA
DATADATADATA
TADATADATADA
DATADATADATA
TADATADATADA
DATADATADATA
TADATADATADA
DATADATADATA
TADATADATADA
DATADATADATA
TADATADATADA

ALLUREALLURE
LUREALLUREAL
REALLUREALLU
ALLUREALLURE
LUREALLUREAL
REALLUREALLU
ALLUREALLURE
LUREALLUREAL
REALLUREALLU
ALLUREALLURE
LUREALLUREAL
REALLUREALLU
ALLUREALLURE
LUREALLUREAL
REALLUREALLU
ALLUREALLURE
LUREALLUREAL
REALLUREALLU
ALLUREALLURE

```
DENDENDENDEN
ENDENDENDEND
DENDENDENDEN
ENDENDENDEND
DENDENDENDEN
ENDENDENDEND
DENDENDENDEN
ENDENDENDEND
DENDENDENDEN
ENDENDENDEND
DENDENDENDEN
ENDENDENDEND
DENDENDENDEN
ENDENDENDEND
DENDENDENDEN
ENDENDENDEND
```

EAREAREAREAR
AREAREAREARE
EAREAREAREAR
AREAREAREARE
EAREAREAREAR
AREAREAREARE
EAREAREAREAR
AREAREAREARE
EAREAREAREAR
AREAREAREARE
EAREAREAREAR
AREAREAREARE
EAREAREAREAR
AREAREAREARE
EAREAREAREAR
AREAREAREARE
EAREAREAREAR
AREAREAREARE
EAREAREAREAR
AREAREAREARE

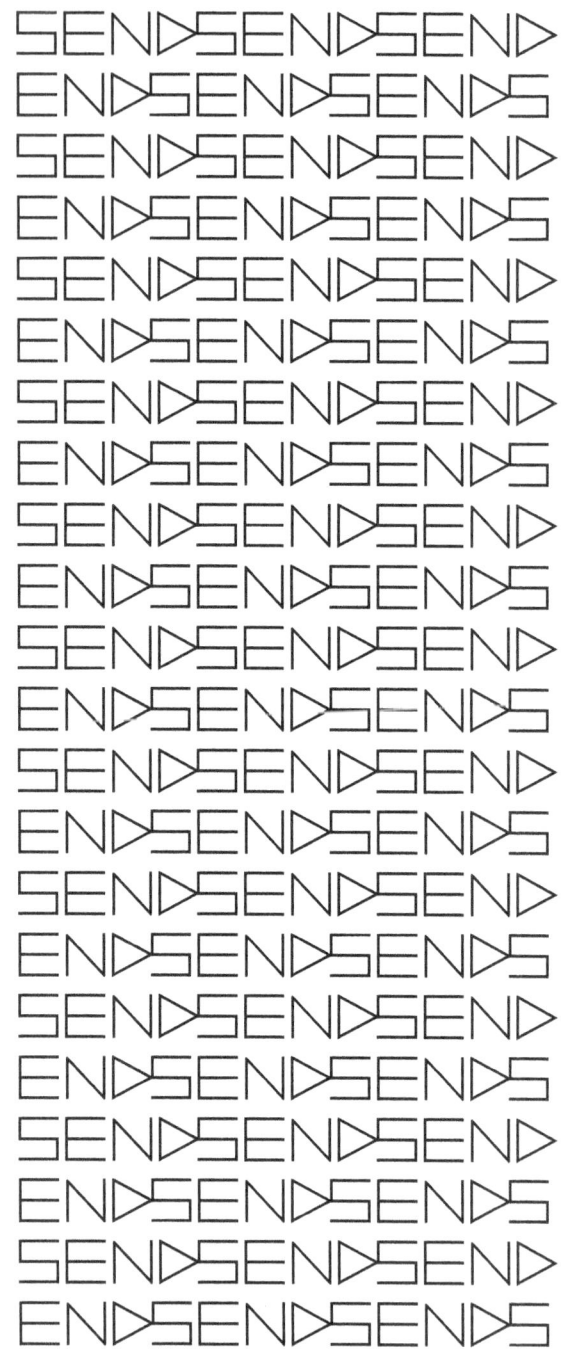

AMAMAM
MAMAMA
AMAMAM
MAMAMA
AMAMAM
MAMAMA
AMAMAM
MAMAMA
AMAMAM
MAMAMA
AMAMAM
MAMAMA
AMAMAM
MAMAMA
AMAMAM
MAMAMA
AMAMAM
MAMAMA
AMAMAM
MAMAMA
AMAMAM
MAMAMA
AMAMAM
MAMAMA
AMAMAM
MAMAMA

ASKEWASKEW
SKEWASKEWA
ASKEWASKEW
SKEWASKEWA
ASKEWASKEW
SKEWASKEWA
ASKEWASKEW
SKEWASKEWA
ASKEWASKEW
SKEWASKEWA
ASKEWASKEW
SKEWASKEWA
ASKEWASKEW
SKEWASKEWA
ASKEWASKEW
SKEWASKEWA
ASKEWASKEW
SKEWASKEWA
ASKEWASKEW
SKEWASKEWA
ASKEWASKEW
SKEWASKEWA

ANEWANEWANEW
WANEWANEWANE
ANEWANEWANEW
WANEWANEWANE
ANEWANEWANEW
WANEWANEWANE
ANEWANEWANEW
WANEWANEWANE
ANEWANEWANEW
WANEWANEWANE
ANEWANEWANEW
WANEWANEWANE
ANEWANEWANEW
WANEWANEWANE
ANEWANEWANEW
WANEWANEWANE
ANEWANEWANEW
WANEWANEWANE
ANEWANEWANEW
WANEWANEWANE

ACTACTACTACT
TACTACTACTAC
ACTACTACTACT
TACTACTACTAC
ACTACTACTACT
TACTACTACTAC
ACTACTACTACT
TACTACTACTAC
ACTACTACTACT
TACTACTACTAC
ACTACTACTACT
TACTACTACTAC
ACTACTACTACT
TACTACTACTAC
ACTACTACTACT
TACTACTACTAC
ACTACTACTACT
TACTACTACTAC
ACTACTACTACT
TACTACTACTAC

LEGALEGALEGA
GALEGALEGALE
EGALEGALEGAL
LEGALEGALEGA
GALEGALEGALE
EGALEGALEGAL
LEGALEGALEGA
GALEGALEGALE
EGALEGALEGAL
LEGALEGALEGA
GALEGALEGALE
EGALEGALEGAL
LEGALEGALEGA
GALEGALEGALE
EGALEGALEGAL
LEGALEGALEGA
GALEGALEGALE
EGALEGALEGAL

HOPSHOPSHOPS
SHOPSHOPSHOP
HOPSHOPSHOPS
SHOPSHOPSHOP
HOPSHOPSHOPS
SHOPSHOPSHOP
HOPSHOPSHOPS
SHOPSHOPSHOP
HOPSHOPSHOPS
SHOPSHOPSHOP
HOPSHOPSHOPS
SHOPSHOPSHOP
HOPSHOPSHOPS
SHOPSHOPSHOP
HOPSHOPSHOPS
SHOPSHOPSHOP
HOPSHOPSHOPS
SHOPSHOPSHOP
HOPSHOPSHOPS
SHOPSHOPSHOP
HOPSHOPSHOPS
SHOPSHOPSHOP
HOPSHOPSHOPS
SHOPSHOPSHOP
HOPSHOPSHOPS
SHOPSHOPSHOP
HOPSHOPSHOPS
SHOPSHOPSHOP

```
IDEAIDEAIDEA
AIDEAIDEAIDE
IDEAIDEAIDEA
AIDEAIDEAIDE
IDEAIDEAIDEA
AIDEAIDEAIDE
IDEAIDEAIDEA
AIDEAIDEAIDE
IDEAIDEAIDEA
AIDEAIDEAIDE
IDEAIDEAIDEA
AIDEAIDEAIDE
IDEAIDEAIDEA
AIDEAIDEAIDE
IDEAIDEAIDEA
AIDEAIDEAIDE
IDEAIDEAIDEA
AIDEAIDEAIDE
IDEAIDEAIDEA
AIDEAIDEAIDE
IDEAIDEAIDEA
AIDEAIDEAIDE
```

ANGERANGER
RANGERANGE
ANGERANGER
RANGERANGE
ANGERANGER
RANGERANGE
ANGERANGER
RANGERANGE
ANGERANGER
RANGERANGE
ANGERANGER
RANGERANGE
ANGERANGER
RANGERANGE
ANGERANGER
RANGERANGE
ANGERANGER
RANGERANGE
ANGERANGER
RANGERANGE

BINGOBINGO
INGOBINGOB
GOBINGOBIN
BINGOBINGO
INGOBINGOB
GOBINGOBIN
BINGOBINGO
INGOBINGOB
GOBINGOBIN
BINGOBINGO
INGOBINGOB
GOBINGOBIN
BINGOBINGO
INGOBINGOB
GOBINGOBIN
BINGOBINGO
INGOBINGOB
GOBINGOBIN
BINGOBINGO
INGOBINGOB
GOBINGOBIN

SEEPAGE
PAGESEE
AGESEEP
SEEPAGE
PAGESEE
AGESEEP
SEEPAGE
PAGESEE
AGESEEP
SEEPAGE
PAGESEE
AGESEEP
SEEPAGE
PAGESEE
AGESEEP
SEEPAGE
PAGESEE
AGESEEP
SEEPAGE
PAGESEE
AGESEEP

PENINSULA
INSULAPEN
LAPENINSU
APENINSUL
PENINSULA
INSULAPEN
LAPENINSU
APENINSUL
PENINSULA
INSULAPEN
LAPENINSU
APENINSUL
PENINSULA
INSULAPEN
LAPENINSU
APENINSUL
PENINSULA
INSULAPEN
LAPENINSU
APENINSUL

LIBIDOLIBIDO
DOLIBIDOLIBI
BIDOLIBIDOLI
LIBIDOLIBIDO
DOLIBIDOLIBI
BIDOLIBIDOLI
LIBIDOLIBIDO
DOLIBIDOLIBI
BIDOLIBIDOLI
LIBIDOLIBIDO
DOLIBIDOLIBI
BIDOLIBIDOLI
LIBIDOLIBIDO
DOLIBIDOLIBI
BIDOLIBIDOLI
LIBIDOLIBIDO
DOLIBIDOLIBI
BIDOLIBIDOLI
LIBIDOLIBIDO
DOLIBIDOLIBI
BIDOLIBIDOLI

ESTATEESTATE
STATEESTATEE
ATEESTATEEST
TEESTATEESTA
ESTATEESTATE
STATEESTATEE
ATEESTATEEST
TEESTATEESTA
ESTATEESTATE
STATEESTATEE
ATEESTATEEST
TEESTATEESTA
ESTATEESTATE
STATEESTATEE
ATEESTATEEST
TEESTATEESTA
ESTATEESTATE
STATEESTATEE
ATEESTATEEST
TEESTATEESTA

INDIGENTINDIGENT
DIGENTINDIGENTIN
GENTINDIGENTINDI
INDIGENTINDIGENT
DIGENTINDIGENTIN
GENTINDIGENTINDI
INDIGENTINDIGENT
DIGENTINDIGENTIN
GENTINDIGENTINDI
INDIGENTINDIGENT
DIGENTINDIGENTIN
GENTINDIGENTINDI
INDIGENTINDIGENT
DIGENTINDIGENTIN
GENTINDIGENTINDI
INDIGENTINDIGENT
DIGENTINDIGENTIN
GENTINDIGENTINDI
INDIGENTINDIGENT
DIGENTINDIGENTIN
GENTINDIGENTINDI

HADESHADES
ADESHADESH
SHADESHADE
HADESHADES
ADESHADESH
SHADESHADE
HADESHADES
ADESHADESH
SHADESHADE
HADESHADES
ADESHADESH
SHADESHADE
HADESHADES
ADESHADESH
SHADESHADE
HADESHADES
ADESHADESH
SHADESHADE
HADESHADES
ADESHADESH
SHADESHADE

INKINKINK
KINKINKIN
INKINKINK
KINKINKIN
INKINKINK
KINKINKIN
INKINKINK
KINKINKIN
INKINKINK
KINKINKIN
INKINKINK
KINKINKIN
INKINKINK
KINKINKIN
INKINKINK
KINKINKIN
INKINKINK
KINKINKIN

ITSITSITS
SITSITSIT
ITSITSITS
SITSITSIT
ITSITSITS
SITSITSIT
ITSITSITS
SITSITSIT
ITSITSITS
SITSITSIT
ITSITSITS
SITSITSIT
ITSITSITS
SITSITSIT
ITSITSITS
SITSITSIT
ITSITSITS
SITSITSIT
ITSITSITS
SITSITSIT
ITSITSITS
SITSITSIT

```
MEGAMEGAMEGA
GAMEGAMEGAME
MEGAMEGAMEGA
GAMEGAMEGAME
MEGAMEGAMEGA
GAMEGAMEGAME
MEGAMEGAMEGA
GAMEGAMEGAME
MEGAMEGAMEGA
GAMEGAMEGAME
MEGAMEGAMEGA
GAMEGAMEGAME
MEGAMEGAMEGA
GAMEGAMEGAME
MEGAMEGAMEGA
GAMEGAMEGAME
MEGAMEGAMEGA
GAMEGAMEGAME
MEGAMEGAMEGA
GAMEGAMEGAME
MEGAMEGAMEGA
GAMEGAMEGAME
MEGAMEGAMEGA
GAMEGAMEGAME
```

ITEMITEMITEM
EMITEMITEMIT
ITEMITEMITEM
EMITEMITEMIT
ITEMITEMITEM
EMITEMITEMIT
ITEMITEMITEM
EMITEMITEMIT
ITEMITEMITEM
EMITEMITEMIT
ITEMITEMITEM
EMITEMITEMIT
ITEMITEMITEM
EMITEMITEMIT
ITEMITEMITEM
EMITEMITEMIT
ITEMITEMITEM
EMITEMITEMIT
ITEMITEMITEM
EMITEMITEMIT
ITEMITEMITEM
EMITEMITEMIT

LEAPLEAPLEAP
PLEAPLEAPLEA
LEAPLEAPLEAP
PLEAPLEAPLEA
LEAPLEAPLEAP
PLEAPLEAPLEA
LEAPLEAPLEAP
PLEAPLEAPLEA
LEAPLEAPLEAP
PLEAPLEAPLEA
LEAPLEAPLEAP
PLEAPLEAPLEA
LEAPLEAPLEAP
PLEAPLEAPLEA
LEAPLEAPLEAP
PLEAPLEAPLEA
LEAPLEAPLEAP
PLEAPLEAPLEA
LEAPLEAPLEAP
PLEAPLEAPLEA

MARMARMAR
ARMARMARM
MARMARMAR
ARMARMARM
MARMARMAR
ARMARMARM
MARMARMAR
ARMARMARM
MARMARMAR
ARMARMARM
MARMARMAR
ARMARMARM
MARMARMAR
ARMARMARM
MARMARMAR
ARMARMARM
MARMARMAR
ARMARMARM
MARMARMAR
ARMARMARM

PLUMPLUM
LUMPLUMP
PLUMPLUM
LUMPLUMP
PLUMPLUM
LUMPLUMP
PLUMPLUM
LUMPLUMP
PLUMPLUM
LUMPLUMP
PLUMPLUM
LUMPLUMP
PLUMPLUM
LUMPLUMP
PLUMPLUM
LUMPLUMP
PLUMPLUM
LUMPLUMP
PLUMPLUM
LUMPLUMP

YOGAYOGA
GAYOGAYO
YOGAYOGA
GAYOGAYO
YOGAYOGA
GAYOGAYO
YOGAYOGA
GAYOGAYO
YOGAYOGA
GAYOGAYO
YOGAYOGA
GAYOGAYO
YOGAYOGA
GAYOGAYO
YOGAYOGA
GAYOGAYO
YOGAYOGA
GAYOGAYO
YOGAYOGA
GAYOGAYO

TIARATIARA
RATIARATIA
TIARATIARA
RATIARATIA
TIARATIARA
RATIARATIA
TIARATIARA
RATIARATIA
TIARATIARA
RATIARATIA
TIARATIARA
RATIARATIA
TIARATIARA
RATIARATIA
TIARATIARA
RATIARATIA
TIARATIARA
RATIARATIA
TIARATIARA
RATIARATIA

ICEDICEDICED
DICEDICEDICE
ICEDICEDICED
DICEDICEDICE
ICEDICEDICED
DICEDICEDICE
ICEDICEDICED
DICEDICEDICE
ICEDICEDICED
DICEDICEDICE
ICEDICEDICED
DICEDICEDICE
ICEDICEDICED
DICEDICEDICE
ICEDICEDICED
DICEDICEDICE
ICEDICEDICED
DICEDICEDICE
ICEDICEDICED
DICEDICEDICE
ICEDICEDICED
DICEDICEDICE
ICEDICEDICED
DICEDICEDICE

MESAMESAMESA
SAMESAMESAME
MESAMESAMESA
SAMESAMESAME
MESAMESAMESA
SAMESAMESAME
MESAMESAMESA
SAMESAMESAME
MESAMESAMESA
SAMESAMESAME
MESAMESAMESA
SAMESAMESAME
MESAMESAMESA
SAMESAMESAME
MESAMESAMESA
SAMESAMESAME
MESAMESAMESA
SAMESAMESAME
MESAMESAMESA
SAMESAMESAME

NONONO
ONONON
NONONO
ONONON
NONONO
ONONON
NONONO
ONONON
NONONO
ONONON
NONONO
ONONON
NONONO
ONONON
NONONO
ONONON
NONONO
ONONON
NONONO
ONONON
NONONO
ONONON
NONONO
ONONON

NOPENOPENOPE
OPENOPENOPEN
NOPENOPENOPE
OPENOPENOPEN
NOPENOPENOPE
OPENOPENOPEN
NOPENOPENOPE
OPENOPENOPEN
NOPENOPENOPE
OPENOPENOPEN
NOPENOPENOPE
OPENOPENOPEN
NOPENOPENOPE
OPENOPENOPEN
NOPENOPENOPE
OPENOPENOPEN
NOPENOPENOPE
OPENOPENOPEN
NOPENOPENOPE
OPENOPENOPEN

SAILSAILSAIL
AILSAILSAILS
SAILSAILSAIL
AILSAILSAILS
SAILSAILSAIL
AILSAILSAILS
SAILSAILSAIL
AILSAILSAILS
SAILSAILSAIL
AILSAILSAILS
SAILSAILSAIL
AILSAILSAILS
SAILSAILSAIL
AILSAILSAILS
SAILSAILSAIL
AILSAILSAILS
SAILSAILSAIL
AILSAILSAILS
SAILSAILSAIL
AILSAILSAILS
SAILSAILSAIL
AILSAILSAILS

OVEROVEROVER
ROVEROVEROVE
OVEROVEROVER
ROVEROVEROVE
OVEROVEROVER
ROVEROVEROVE
OVEROVEROVER
ROVEROVEROVE
OVEROVEROVER
ROVEROVEROVE
OVEROVEROVER
ROVEROVEROVE
OVEROVEROVER
ROVEROVEROVE
OVEROVEROVER
ROVEROVEROVE
OVEROVEROVER
ROVEROVEROVE
OVEROVEROVER
ROVEROVEROVE

RELYRELYRELY
LYRELYRELYRE
RELYRELYRELY
LYRELYRELYRE
RELYRELYRELY
LYRELYRELYRE
RELYRELYRELY
LYRELYRELYRE
RELYRELYRELY
LYRELYRELYRE
RELYRELYRELY
LYRELYRELYRE
RELYRELYRELY
LYRELYRELYRE
RELYRELYRELY
LYRELYRELYRE
RELYRELYRELY
LYRELYRELYRE

OPTOPTOPT
POTPOTPOT
OPTOPTOPT
POTPOTPOT
OPTOPTOPT
POTPOTPOT
OPTOPTOPT
POTPOTPOT
OPTOPTOPT
POTPOTPOT
OPTOPTOPT
POTPOTPOT
OPTOPTOPT
POTPOTPOT
OPTOPTOPT
POTPOTPOT
OPTOPTOPT
POTPOTPOT
OPTOPTOPT
POTPOTPOT
OPTOPTOPT
POTPOTPOT
OPTOPTOPT
POTPOTPOT

TANTANTAN
ANTANTANT
TANTANTAN
ANTANTANT
TANTANTAN
ANTANTANT
TANTANTAN
ANTANTANT
TANTANTAN
ANTANTANT
TANTANTAN
ANTANTANT
TANTANTAN
ANTANTANT
TANTANTAN
ANTANTANT
TANTANTAN
ANTANTANT

TYPETYPETYPE
PETYPETYPETY
TYPETYPETYPE
PETYPETYPETY
TYPETYPETYPE
PETYPETYPETY
TYPETYPETYPE
PETYPETYPETY
TYPETYPETYPE
PETYPETYPETY
TYPETYPETYPE
PETYPETYPETY
TYPETYPETYPE
PETYPETYPETY
TYPETYPETYPE
PETYPETYPETY
TYPETYPETYPE
PETYPETYPETY
TYPETYPETYPE
PETYPETYPETY
TYPETYPETYPE
PETYPETYPETY

WHOWHOWHO
HOWHOWHOW
WHOWHOWHO
HOWHOWHOW
WHOWHOWHO
HOWHOWHOW
WHOWHOWHO
HOWHOWHOW
WHOWHOWHO
HOWHOWHOW
WHOWHOWHO
HOWHOWHOW
WHOWHOWHO
HOWHOWHOW
WHOWHOWHO
HOWHOWHOW
WHOWHOWHO
HOWHOWHOW
WHOWHOWHO
HOWHOWHOW

TRAITSTRAITS
STRAITSTRAIT
TRAITSTRAITS
STRAITSTRAIT
TRAITSTRAITS
STRAITSTRAIT
TRAITSTRAITS
STRAITSTRAIT
TRAITSTRAITS
STRAITSTRAIT
TRAITSTRAITS
STRAITSTRAIT
TRAITSTRAITS
STRAITSTRAIT
TRAITSTRAITS
STRAITSTRAIT
TRAITSTRAITS
STRAITSTRAIT
TRAITSTRAITS
STRAITSTRAIT

ownownown
nownownow
ownownown
nownownow
ownownown
nownownow
ownownown
nownownow
ownownown
nownownow
ownownown
nownownow
ownownown
nownownow
ownownown
nownownow
ownownown
nownownow

SCREWSCREW
CREWSCREWS
SCREWSCREW
CREWSCREWS
SCREWSCREW
CREWSCREWS
SCREWSCREW
CREWSCREWS
SCREWSCREW
CREWSCREWS
SCREWSCREW
CREWSCREWS
SCREWSCREW
CREWSCREWS
SCREWSCREW
CREWSCREWS
SCREWSCREW
CREWSCREWS
SCREWSCREW
CREWSCREWS
SCREWSCREW
CREWSCREWS

STORESTORE
RESTORESTO
STORESTORE
RESTORESTO
STORESTORE
RESTORESTO
STORESTORE
RESTORESTO
STORESTORE
RESTORESTO
STORESTORE
RESTORESTO
STORESTORE
RESTORESTO
STORESTORE
RESTORESTO
STORESTORE
RESTORESTO
STORESTORE
RESTORESTO
STORESTORE
RESTORESTO
STORESTORE
RESTORESTO

UTTERUTTER
RUTTERUTTE
UTTERUTTER
RUTTERUTTE
UTTERUTTER
RUTTERUTTE
UTTERUTTER
RUTTERUTTE
UTTERUTTER
RUTTERUTTE
UTTERUTTER
RUTTERUTTE
UTTERUTTER
RUTTERUTTE
UTTERUTTER
RUTTERUTTE
UTTERUTTER
RUTTERUTTE
UTTERUTTER
RUTTERUTTE
UTTERUTTER
RUTTERUTTE

APARTAPART
PARTAPARTA
APARTAPART
PARTAPARTA
APARTAPART
PARTAPARTA
APARTAPART
PARTAPARTA
APARTAPART
PARTAPARTA
APARTAPART
PARTAPARTA
APARTAPART
PARTAPARTA
APARTAPART
PARTAPARTA
APARTAPART
PARTAPARTA
APARTAPART
PARTAPARTA

FARFARFARFAR
ARFARFARFARF
FARFARFARFAR
ARFARFARFARF
FARFARFARFAR
ARFARFARFARF
FARFARFARFAR
ARFARFARFARF
FARFARFARFAR
ARFARFARFARF
FARFARFARFAR
ARFARFARFARF
FARFARFARFAR
ARFARFARFARF
FARFARFARFAR
ARFARFARFARF
FARFARFARFAR
ARFARFARFARF
FARFARFARFAR
ARFARFARFARF

EARLYEARLY
YEARLYEARL
EARLYEARLY
YEARLYEARL
EARLYEARLY
YEARLYEARL
EARLYEARLY
YEARLYEARL
EARLYEARLY
YEARLYEARL
EARLYEARLY
YEARLYEARL
EARLYEARLY
YEARLYEARL
EARLYEARLY
YEARLYEARL
EARLYEARLY
YEARLYEARL

EARTHEARTH
HEARTHEART
EARTHEARTH
HEARTHEART
EARTHEARTH
HEARTHEART
EARTHEARTH
HEARTHEART
EARTHEARTH
HEARTHEART
EARTHEARTH
HEARTHEART
EARTHEARTH
HEARTHEART
EARTHEARTH
HEARTHEART
EARTHEARTH
HEARTHEART
EARTHEARTH
HEARTHEART

STONESTONE
TONESTONES
ONESTONEST
STONESTONE
TONESTONES
ONESTONEST
STONESTONE
TONESTONES
ONESTONEST
STONESTONE
TONESTONES
ONESTONEST
STONESTONE
TONESTONES
ONESTONEST
STONESTONE
TONESTONES
ONESTONEST
STONESTONE
TONESTONES
ONESTONEST

ONEONE
NEONEO
EONEON
ONEONE
NEONEO
EONEON
ONEONE
NEONEO
EONEON
ONEONE
NEONEO
EONEON
ONEONE
NEONEO
EONEON
ONEONE
NEONEO
EONEON
ONEONE
NEONEO
EONEON

SEEPAGESEEPAGE
PAGESEEPAGESEE
SEEPAGESEEPAGE
PAGESEEPAGESEE
SEEPAGESEEPAGE
PAGESEEPAGESEE
SEEPAGESEEPAGE
PAGESEEPAGESEE
SEEPAGESEEPAGE
PAGESEEPAGESEE
SEEPAGESEEPAGE
PAGESEEPAGESEE
SEEPAGESEEPAGE
PAGESEEPAGESEE
SEEPAGESEEPAGE
PAGESEEPAGESEE
SEEPAGESEEPAGE
PAGESEEPAGESEE
SEEPAGESEEPAGE
PAGESEEPAGESEE
SEEPAGESEEPAGE
PAGESEEPAGESEE
SEEPAGESEEPAGE
PAGESEEPAGESEE

TEATEATEA
ATEATEATE
EATEATEAT
TEATEATEA
ATEATEATE
EATEATEAT
TEATEATEA
ATEATEATE
EATEATEAT
TEATEATEA
ATEATEATE
EATEATEAT
TEATEATEA
ATEATEATE
EATEATEAT
TEATEATEA
ATEATEATE
EATEATEAT
TEATEATEA
ATEATEATE
EATEATEAT

FREEREEFFREEREEF
REEFREEREEFFREE
FREEREEFFREEREEF
REEFREEREEFFREE
FREEREEFFREEREEF
REEFREEREEFFREE
FREEREEFFREEREEF
REEFREEREEFFREE
FREEREEFFREEREEF
REEFREEREEFFREE
FREEREEFFREEREEF
REEFREEREEFFREE
FREEREEFFREEREEF
REEFREEREEFFREE
FREEREEFFREEREEF
REEFREEREEFFREE
FREEREEFFREEREEF
REEFREEREEFFREE
FREEREEFFREEREEF
REEFREEREEFFREE

PEAPEAPEAPEA
APEAPEAPEAPE
PEAPEAPEAPEA
APEAPEAPEAPE
PEAPEAPEAPEA
APEAPEAPEAPE
PEAPEAPEAPEA
APEAPEAPEAPE
PEAPEAPEAPEA
APEAPEAPEAPE
PEAPEAPEAPEA
APEAPEAPEAPE
PEAPEAPEAPEA
APEAPEAPEAPE
PEAPEAPEAPEA
APEAPEAPEAPE
PEAPEAPEAPEA
APEAPEAPEAPE
PEAPEAPEAPEA
APEAPEAPEAPE
PEAPEAPEAPEA
APEAPEAPEAPE
PEAPEAPEAPEA
APEAPEAPEAPE
PEAPEAPEAPEA
APEAPEAPEAPE
PEAPEAPEAPEA
APEAPEAPEAPE
PEAPEAPEAPEA
APEAPEAPEAPE

OAROAROAROAR
ROAROAROAROA
OAROAROAROAR
ROAROAROAROA
OAROAROAROAR
ROAROAROAROA
OAROAROAROAR
ROAROAROAROA
OAROAROAROAR
ROAROAROAROA
OAROAROAROAR
ROAROAROAROA
OAROAROAROAR
ROAROAROAROA
OAROAROAROAR
ROAROAROAROA
OAROAROAROAR
ROAROAROAROA
OAROAROAROAR
ROAROAROAROA
OAROAROAROAR
ROAROAROAROA
OAROAROAROAR
ROAROAROAROA
OAROAROAROAR
ROAROAROAROA
OAROAROAROAR
ROAROAROAROA
OAROAROAROAR
ROAROAROAROA

IMPIMPIMPIMP
PIMPIMPIMPIM
IMPIMPIMPIMP
PIMPIMPIMPIM
IMPIMPIMPIMP
PIMPIMPIMPIM
IMPIMPIMPIMP
PIMPIMPIMPIM
IMPIMPIMPIMP
PIMPIMPIMPIM
IMPIMPIMPIMP
PIMPIMPIMPIM
IMPIMPIMPIMP
PIMPIMPIMPIM
IMPIMPIMPIMP
PIMPIMPIMPIM
IMPIMPIMPIMP
PIMPIMPIMPIM
IMPIMPIMPIMP
PIMPIMPIMPIM
IMPIMPIMPIMP
PIMPIMPIMPIM
IMPIMPIMPIMP
PIMPIMPIMPIM
IMPIMPIMPIMP
PIMPIMPIMPIM
IMPIMPIMPIMP
PIMPIMPIMPIM
IMPIMPIMPIMP
PIMPIMPIMPIM
IMPIMPIMPIMP
PIMPIMPIMPIM

EROSEROSEROS
ROSEROSEROSE
EROSEROSEROS
ROSEROSEROSE
EROSEROSEROS
ROSEROSEROSE
EROSEROSEROS
ROSEROSEROSE
EROSEROSEROS
ROSEROSEROSE
EROSEROSEROS
ROSEROSEROSE
EROSEROSEROS
ROSEROSEROSE
EROSEROSEROS
ROSEROSEROSE
EROSEROSEROS
ROSEROSEROSE
EROSEROSEROS
ROSEROSEROSE
EROSEROSEROS
ROSEROSEROSE
EROSEROSEROS
ROSEROSEROSE
EROSEROSEROS
ROSEROSEROSE

```
RICERICERICE
ICERICERICER
RICERICERICE
ICERICERICER
RICERICERICE
ICERICERICER
RICERICERICE
ICERICERICER
RICERICERICE
ICERICERICER
RICERICERICE
ICERICERICER
RICERICERICE
ICERICERICER
RICERICERICE
ICERICERICER
RICERICERICE
ICERICERICER
RICERICERICE
ICERICERICER
RICERICERICE
ICERICERICER
RICERICERICE
ICERICERICER
```

DIREDIREDIRE
REDIREDIREDI
DIREDIREDIRE
REDIREDIREDI
DIREDIREDIRE
REDIREDIREDI
DIREDIREDIRE
REDIREDIREDI
DIREDIREDIRE
REDIREDIREDI
DIREDIREDIRE
REDIREDIREDI
DIREDIREDIRE
REDIREDIREDI
DIREDIREDIRE
REDIREDIREDI
DIREDIREDIRE
REDIREDIREDI
DIREDIREDIRE
REDIREDIREDI
DIREDIREDIRE
REDIREDIREDI
DIREDIREDIRE
REDIREDIREDI

LEASELEASELEASE
EASELEASELEASEL
LEASELEASELEASE
EASELEASELEASEL
LEASELEASELEASE
EASELEASELEASEL
LEASELEASELEASE
EASELEASELEASEL
LEASELEASELEASE
EASELEASELEASEL
LEASELEASELEASE
EASELEASELEASEL
LEASELEASELEASE
EASELEASELEASEL
LEASELEASELEASE
EASELEASELEASEL
LEASELEASELEASE
EASELEASELEASEL
LEASELEASELEASE
EASELEASELEASEL

OVERBOARDOVERBOARD
DOVERBOARDOVERBOAR
BOARDOVERBOARDOVER
OVERBOARDOVERBOARD
DOVERBOARDOVERBOAR
BOARDOVERBOARDOVER
OVERBOARDOVERBOARD
DOVERBOARDOVERBOAR
BOARDOVERBOARDOVER
OVERBOARDOVERBOARD
DOVERBOARDOVERBOAR
BOARDOVERBOARDOVER
OVERBOARDOVERBOARD
DOVERBOARDOVERBOAR
BOARDOVERBOARDOVER
OVERBOARDOVERBOARD
DOVERBOARDOVERBOAR
BOARDOVERBOARDOVER
OVERBOARDOVERBOARD
DOVERBOARDOVERBOAR
BOARDOVERBOARDOVER

SONARSONAR
ARSONARSON
SONARSONAR
ARSONARSON
SONARSONAR
ARSONARSON
SONARSONAR
ARSONARSON
SONARSONAR
ARSONARSON
SONARSONAR
ARSONARSON
SONARSONAR
ARSONARSON
SONARSONAR
ARSONARSON
SONARSONAR
ARSONARSON
SONARSONAR
ARSONARSON

ENTERTAINMENT
MENTENTERTAIN
TENTERTAINMEN
ENTERTAINMENT
MENTENTERTAIN
TENTERTAINMEN
ENTERTAINMENT
MENTENTERTAIN
TENTERTAINMEN
ENTERTAINMENT
MENTENTERTAIN
TENTERTAINMEN
ENTERTAINMENT
MENTENTERTAIN
TENTERTAINMEN
ENTERTAINMENT
MENTENTERTAIN
TENTERTAINMEN
ENTERTAINMENT
MENTENTERTAIN
TENTERTAINMEN

INJUSTICEINJUSTICE
JUSTICEINJUSTICEIN
ICEINJUSTICEINJUST
INJUSTICEINJUSTICE
JUSTICEINJUSTICEIN
ICEINJUSTICEINJUST
INJUSTICEINJUSTICE
JUSTICEINJUSTICEIN
ICEINJUSTICEINJUST
INJUSTICEINJUSTICE
JUSTICEINJUSTICEIN
ICEINJUSTICEINJUST
INJUSTICEINJUSTICE
JUSTICEINJUSTICEIN
ICEINJUSTICEINJUST
INJUSTICEINJUSTICE
JUSTICEINJUSTICEIN
ICEINJUSTICEINJUST
INJUSTICEINJUSTICE
JUSTICEINJUSTICEIN
ICEINJUSTICEINJUST

EARLIESTEARLIEST
TEARLIESTEARLIES
LIESTEARLIESTEAR
EARLIESTEARLIEST
TEARLIESTEARLIES
LIESTEARLIESTEAR
EARLIESTEARLIEST
TEARLIESTEARLIES
LIESTEARLIESTEAR
EARLIESTEARLIEST
TEARLIESTEARLIES
LIESTEARLIESTEAR
EARLIESTEARLIEST
TEARLIESTEARLIES
LIESTEARLIESTEAR
EARLIESTEARLIEST
TEARLIESTEARLIES
LIESTEARLIESTEAR
EARLIESTEARLIEST
TEARLIESTEARLIES
LIESTEARLIESTEAR
EARLIESTEARLIEST
TEARLIESTEARLIES
LIESTEARLIESTEAR

EPISODEEPISODE
DEEPISODEEPISO
ISODEEPISODEEP
EPISODEEPISODE
DEEPISODEEPISO
ISODEEPISODEEP
EPISODEEPISODE
DEEPISODEEPISO
ISODEEPISODEEP
EPISODEEPISODE
DEEPISODEEPISO
ISODEEPISODEEP
EPISODEEPISODE
DEEPISODEEPISO
ISODEEPISODEEP
EPISODEEPISODE
DEEPISODEEPISO
ISODEEPISODEEP
EPISODEEPISODE
DEEPISODEEPISO
ISODEEPISODEEP
EPISODEEPISODE
DEEPISODEEPISO
ISODEEPISODEEP

INSIGNIFICANTINSIGNIFICANT
TINSIGNIFICANTINSIGNIFICAN
SIGNIFICANTINSIGNIFICANTIN
IFICANTINSIGNIFICANTINSIGN
ICANTINSIGNIFICANTINSIGNIF
INSIGNIFICANTINSIGNIFICANT
TINSIGNIFICANTINSIGNIFICAN
SIGNIFICANTINSIGNIFICANTIN
IFICANTINSIGNIFICANTINSIGN
ICANTINSIGNIFICANTINSIGNIF
INSIGNIFICANTINSIGNIFICANT
TINSIGNIFICANTINSIGNIFICAN
SIGNIFICANTINSIGNIFICANTIN
IFICANTINSIGNIFICANTINSIGN
ICANTINSIGNIFICANTINSIGNIF
INSIGNIFICANTINSIGNIFICANT
TINSIGNIFICANTINSIGNIFICAN
SIGNIFICANTINSIGNIFICANTIN
IFICANTINSIGNIFICANTINSIGN
ICANTINSIGNIFICANTINSIGNIF
INSIGNIFICANTINSIGNIFICANT
TINSIGNIFICANTINSIGNIFICAN
SIGNIFICANTINSIGNIFICANTIN
IFICANTINSIGNIFICANTINSIGN
ICANTINSIGNIFICANTINSIGNIF
INSIGNIFICANTINSIGNIFICANT
TINSIGNIFICANTINSIGNIFICAN
SIGNIFICANTINSIGNIFICANTIN
IFICANTINSIGNIFICANTINSIGN
ICANTINSIGNIFICANTINSIGNIF
INSIGNIFICANTINSIGNIFICANT
TINSIGNIFICANTINSIGNIFICAN
SIGNIFICANTINSIGNIFICANTIN

ESTRANGEMENTESTRANGEMENT
TESTRANGEMENTESTRANGEMEN
MENTESTRANGEMENTESTRANGE
ESTRANGEMENTESTRANGEMENT
TESTRANGEMENTESTRANGEMEN
MENTESTRANGEMENTESTRANGE
ESTRANGEMENTESTRANGEMENT
TESTRANGEMENTESTRANGEMEN
MENTESTRANGEMENTESTRANGE
ESTRANGEMENTESTRANGEMENT
TESTRANGEMENTESTRANGEMEN
MENTESTRANGEMENTESTRANGE
ESTRANGEMENTESTRANGEMENT
TESTRANGEMENTESTRANGEMEN
MENTESTRANGEMENTESTRANGE
ESTRANGEMENTESTRANGEMENT
TESTRANGEMENTESTRANGEMEN
MENTESTRANGEMENTESTRANGE
ESTRANGEMENTESTRANGEMENT
TESTRANGEMENTESTRANGEMEN
MENTESTRANGEMENTESTRANGE
ESTRANGEMENTESTRANGEMENT
TESTRANGEMENTESTRANGEMEN
MENTESTRANGEMENTESTRANGE
ESTRANGEMENTESTRANGEMENT
TESTRANGEMENTESTRANGEMEN
MENTESTRANGEMENTESTRANGE
ESTRANGEMENTESTRANGEMENT
TESTRANGEMENTESTRANGEMEN
MENTESTRANGEMENTESTRANGE

CHANTMENTENCHANTMENTEN
ENCHANTMENTENCHANTMENT
TENCHANTMENTENCHANTMEN
CHANTMENTENCHANTMENTEN
ENCHANTMENTENCHANTMENT
TENCHANTMENTENCHANTMEN
CHANTMENTENCHANTMENTEN
ENCHANTMENTENCHANTMENT
TENCHANTMENTENCHANTMEN
CHANTMENTENCHANTMENTEN
ENCHANTMENTENCHANTMENT
TENCHANTMENTENCHANTMEN
CHANTMENTENCHANTMENTEN
ENCHANTMENTENCHANTMENT
TENCHANTMENTENCHANTMEN
CHANTMENTENCHANTMENTEN
ENCHANTMENTENCHANTMENT
TENCHANTMENTENCHANTMEN
CHANTMENTENCHANTMENTEN
ENCHANTMENTENCHANTMENT
TENCHANTMENTENCHANTMEN
CHANTMENTENCHANTMENTEN
ENCHANTMENTENCHANTMENT
TENCHANTMENTENCHANTMEN
CHANTMENTENCHANTMENTEN
ENCHANTMENTENCHANTMENT
TENCHANTMENTENCHANTMEN

RAPISTRAPISTRAPIST
TRAPISTRAPISTRAPIS
ISTRAPISTRAPISTRAP
RAPISTRAPISTRAPIST
TRAPISTRAPISTRAPIS
ISTRAPISTRAPISTRAP
RAPISTRAPISTRAPIST
TRAPISTRAPISTRAPIS
ISTRAPISTRAPISTRAP
RAPISTRAPISTRAPIST
TRAPISTRAPISTRAPIS
ISTRAPISTRAPISTRAP
RAPISTRAPISTRAPIST
TRAPISTRAPISTRAPIS
ISTRAPISTRAPISTRAP
RAPISTRAPISTRAPIST
TRAPISTRAPISTRAPIS
ISTRAPISTRAPISTRAP
RAPISTRAPISTRAPIST
TRAPISTRAPISTRAPIS
ISTRAPISTRAPISTRAP
RAPISTRAPISTRAPIST
TRAPISTRAPISTRAPIS
ISTRAPISTRAPISTRAP
RAPISTRAPISTRAPIST
TRAPISTRAPISTRAPIS
ISTRAPISTRAPISTRAP
RAPISTRAPISTRAPIST
TRAPISTRAPISTRAPIS
ISTRAPISTRAPISTRAP

PASTAPASTAPASTA
ASTAPASTAPASTAP
TAPASTAPASTAPAS
PASTAPASTAPASTA
ASTAPASTAPASTAP
TAPASTAPASTAPAS
PASTAPASTAPASTA
ASTAPASTAPASTAP
TAPASTAPASTAPAS
PASTAPASTAPASTA
ASTAPASTAPASTAP
TAPASTAPASTAPAS
PASTAPASTAPASTA
ASTAPASTAPASTAP
TAPASTAPASTAPAS
PASTAPASTAPASTA
ASTAPASTAPASTAP
TAPASTAPASTAPAS
PASTAPASTAPASTA
ASTAPASTAPASTAP
TAPASTAPASTAPAS
PASTAPASTAPASTA
ASTAPASTAPASTAP
TAPASTAPASTAPAS
PASTAPASTAPASTA
ASTAPASTAPASTAP
TAPASTAPASTAPAS

OTHEROTHEROTHER
THEROTHEROTHERO
HEROTHEROTHEROT
ROTHEROTHEROTHE
OTHEROTHEROTHER
THEROTHEROTHERO
HEROTHEROTHEROT
ROTHEROTHEROTHE
OTHEROTHEROTHER
THEROTHEROTHERO
HEROTHEROTHEROT
ROTHEROTHEROTHE
OTHEROTHEROTHER
THEROTHEROTHERO
HEROTHEROTHEROT
ROTHEROTHEROTHE
OTHEROTHEROTHER
THEROTHEROTHERO
HEROTHEROTHEROT
ROTHEROTHEROTHE
OTHEROTHEROTHER
THEROTHEROTHERO
HEROTHEROTHEROT
ROTHEROTHEROTHE
OTHEROTHEROTHER
THEROTHEROTHERO
HEROTHEROTHEROT
ROTHEROTHEROTHE

INDIGENTINDIGENTINDIGENT
DIGENTINDIGENTINDIGENTIN
GENTINDIGENTINDIGENTINDI
INDIGENTINDIGENTINDIGENT
DIGENTINDIGENTINDIGENTIN
GENTINDIGENTINDIGENTINDI
INDIGENTINDIGENTINDIGENT
DIGENTINDIGENTINDIGENTIN
GENTINDIGENTINDIGENTINDI
INDIGENTINDIGENTINDIGENT
DIGENTINDIGENTINDIGENTIN
GENTINDIGENTINDIGENTINDI
INDIGENTINDIGENTINDIGENT
DIGENTINDIGENTINDIGENTIN
GENTINDIGENTINDIGENTINDI
INDIGENTINDIGENTINDIGENT
DIGENTINDIGENTINDIGENTIN
GENTINDIGENTINDIGENTINDI
INDIGENTINDIGENTINDIGENT
DIGENTINDIGENTINDIGENTIN
GENTINDIGENTINDIGENTINDI
INDIGENTINDIGENTINDIGENT
DIGENTINDIGENTINDIGENTIN
GENTINDIGENTINDIGENTINDI
INDIGENTINDIGENTINDIGENT
DIGENTINDIGENTINDIGENTIN
GENTINDIGENTINDIGENTINDI
INDIGENTINDIGENTINDIGENT
DIGENTINDIGENTINDIGENTIN
GENTINDIGENTINDIGENTINDI

APOTHEOSISAPOTHEOSIS
POTHEOSISAPOTHEOSISA
THEOSISAPOTHEOSISAPO
HEOSISAPOTHEOSISAPOT
ISAPOTHEOSISAPOTHEOS
APOTHEOSISAPOTHEOSIS
POTHEOSISAPOTHEOSISA
THEOSISAPOTHEOSISAPO
HEOSISAPOTHEOSISAPOT
ISAPOTHEOSISAPOTHEOS
APOTHEOSISAPOTHEOSIS
POTHEOSISAPOTHEOSISA
THEOSISAPOTHEOSISAPO
HEOSISAPOTHEOSISAPOT
ISAPOTHEOSISAPOTHEOS
APOTHEOSISAPOTHEOSIS
POTHEOSISAPOTHEOSISA
THEOSISAPOTHEOSISAPO
HEOSISAPOTHEOSISAPOT
ISAPOTHEOSISAPOTHEOS
APOTHEOSISAPOTHEOSIS
POTHEOSISAPOTHEOSISA
THEOSISAPOTHEOSISAPO
HEOSISAPOTHEOSISAPOT
ISAPOTHEOSISAPOTHEOS
APOTHEOSISAPOTHEOSIS
POTHEOSISAPOTHEOSISA
THEOSISAPOTHEOSISAPO
HEOSISAPOTHEOSISAPOT
ISAPOTHEOSISAPOTHEOS

EPHEMERALEPHEMERAL
ALEPHEMERALEPHEMER
ERALEPHEMERALEPHEM
EPHEMERALEPHEMERAL
ALEPHEMERALEPHEMER
ERALEPHEMERALEPHEM
EPHEMERALEPHEMERAL
ALEPHEMERALEPHEMER
ERALEPHEMERALEPHEM
EPHEMERALEPHEMERAL
ALEPHEMERALEPHEMER
ERALEPHEMERALEPHEM
EPHEMERALEPHEMERAL
ALEPHEMERALEPHEMER
ERALEPHEMERALEPHEM
EPHEMERALEPHEMERAL
ALEPHEMERALEPHEMER
ERALEPHEMERALEPHEM
EPHEMERALEPHEMERAL
ALEPHEMERALEPHEMER
ERALEPHEMERALEPHEM
EPHEMERALEPHEMERAL
ALEPHEMERALEPHEMER
ERALEPHEMERALEPHEM
EPHEMERALEPHEMERAL
ALEPHEMERALEPHEMER
ERALEPHEMERALEPHEM
EPHEMERALEPHEMERAL
ALEPHEMERALEPHEMER
ERALEPHEMERALEPHEM

APOTHEOSISAPOTHEOSIS
POTHEOSISAPOTHEOSISA
THEOSISAPOTHEOSISAPO
HEOSISAPOTHEOSISAPOT
ISAPOTHEOSISAPOTHEOS
APOTHEOSISAPOTHEOSIS
POTHEOSISAPOTHEOSISA
THEOSISAPOTHEOSISAPO
HEOSISAPOTHEOSISAPOT
ISAPOTHEOSISAPOTHEOS
APOTHEOSISAPOTHEOSIS
POTHEOSISAPOTHEOSISA
THEOSISAPOTHEOSISAPO
HEOSISAPOTHEOSISAPOT
ISAPOTHEOSISAPOTHEOS
APOTHEOSISAPOTHEOSIS
POTHEOSISAPOTHEOSISA
THEOSISAPOTHEOSISAPO
HEOSISAPOTHEOSISAPOT
ISAPOTHEOSISAPOTHEOS

OVERALLOVERALL
LOVERALLOVERAL
ALLOVERALLOVER
OVERALLOVERALL
LOVERALLOVERAL
ALLOVERALLOVER
OVERALLOVERALL
LOVERALLOVERAL
ALLOVERALLOVER
OVERALLOVERALL
LOVERALLOVERAL
ALLOVERALLOVER
OVERALLOVERALL
LOVERALLOVERAL
ALLOVERALLOVER
OVERALLOVERALL
LOVERALLOVERAL
ALLOVERALLOVER
OVERALLOVERALL
LOVERALLOVERAL
ALLOVERALLOVER

ONSLAUGHTONSLAUGHT
LAUGHTONSLAUGHTONS
TONSLAUGHTONSLAUGH
ONSLAUGHTONSLAUGHT
LAUGHTONSLAUGHTONS
TONSLAUGHTONSLAUGH
ONSLAUGHTONSLAUGHT
LAUGHTONSLAUGHTONS
TONSLAUGHTONSLAUGH
ONSLAUGHTONSLAUGHT
LAUGHTONSLAUGHTONS
TONSLAUGHTONSLAUGH
ONSLAUGHTONSLAUGHT
LAUGHTONSLAUGHTONS
TONSLAUGHTONSLAUGH
ONSLAUGHTONSLAUGHT
LAUGHTONSLAUGHTONS
TONSLAUGHTONSLAUGH
ONSLAUGHTONSLAUGHT
LAUGHTONSLAUGHTONS
TONSLAUGHTONSLAUGH

ETHEREALETHEREAL
THEREALETHEREALE
REALETHEREALETHE
ETHEREALETHEREAL
THEREALETHEREALE
REALETHEREALETHE
ETHEREALETHEREAL
THEREALETHEREALE
REALETHEREALETHE
ETHEREALETHEREAL
THEREALETHEREALE
REALETHEREALETHE
ETHEREALETHEREAL
THEREALETHEREALE
REALETHEREALETHE
ETHEREALETHEREAL
THEREALETHEREALE
REALETHEREALETHE

INSIGHTINSIGHT
TINSIGHTINSIGH
SIGHTINSIGHTIN
INSIGHTINSIGHT
TINSIGHTINSIGH
SIGHTINSIGHTIN
INSIGHTINSIGHT
TINSIGHTINSIGH
SIGHTINSIGHTIN
INSIGHTINSIGHT
TINSIGHTINSIGH
SIGHTINSIGHTIN
INSIGHTINSIGHT
TINSIGHTINSIGH
SIGHTINSIGHTIN
INSIGHTINSIGHT
TINSIGHTINSIGH
SIGHTINSIGHTIN
INSIGHTINSIGHT
TINSIGHTINSIGH
SIGHTINSIGHTIN

UNDERDOGUNDERDOG
GUNDERDOGUNDERDO
DOGUNDERDOGUNDER
UNDERDOGUNDERDOG
GUNDERDOGUNDERDO
DOGUNDERDOGUNDER
UNDERDOGUNDERDOG
GUNDERDOGUNDERDO
DOGUNDERDOGUNDER
UNDERDOGUNDERDOG
GUNDERDOGUNDERDO
DOGUNDERDOGUNDER
UNDERDOGUNDERDOG
GUNDERDOGUNDERDO
DOGUNDERDOGUNDER
UNDERDOGUNDERDOG
GUNDERDOGUNDERDO
DOGUNDERDOGUNDER
UNDERDOGUNDERDOG
GUNDERDOGUNDERDO
DOGUNDERDOGUNDER

ORDEALORDEAL
LORDEALORDEA
DEALORDEALOR
ORDEALORDEAL
LORDEALORDEA
DEALORDEALOR
ORDEALORDEAL
LORDEALORDEA
DEALORDEALOR
ORDEALORDEAL
LORDEALORDEA
DEALORDEALOR
ORDEALORDEAL
LORDEALORDEA
DEALORDEALOR
ORDEALORDEAL
LORDEALORDEA
DEALORDEALOR
ORDEALORDEAL
LORDEALORDEA
DEALORDEALOR

ENTHUSIASMENTHUSIASM
MENTHUSIASMENTHUSIAS
USIASMENTHUSIASMENTH
ENTHUSIASMENTHUSIASM
MENTHUSIASMENTHUSIAS
USIASMENTHUSIASMENTH
ENTHUSIASMENTHUSIASM
MENTHUSIASMENTHUSIAS
USIASMENTHUSIASMENTH
ENTHUSIASMENTHUSIASM
MENTHUSIASMENTHUSIAS
USIASMENTHUSIASMENTH
ENTHUSIASMENTHUSIASM
MENTHUSIASMENTHUSIAS
USIASMENTHUSIASMENTH
ENTHUSIASMENTHUSIASM
MENTHUSIASMENTHUSIAS
USIASMENTHUSIASMENTH
ENTHUSIASMENTHUSIASM
MENTHUSIASMENTHUSIAS
USIASMENTHUSIASMENTH

HESITATESHESITATES
SHESITATESHESITATE
SITATESHESITATESHE
ATESHESITATESHESIT
HESITATESHESITATES
SHESITATESHESITATE
SITATESHESITATESHE
ATESHESITATESHESIT
HESITATESHESITATES
SHESITATESHESITATE
SITATESHESITATESHE
ATESHESITATESHESIT
HESITATESHESITATES
SHESITATESHESITATE
SITATESHESITATESHE
ATESHESITATESHESIT
HESITATESHESITATES
SHESITATESHESITATE
SITATESHESITATESHE
ATESHESITATESHESIT

ANTHEMANTHEM
THEMANTHEMAN
MANTHEMANTHE
ANTHEMANTHEM
THEMANTHEMAN
MANTHEMANTHE
ANTHEMANTHEM
THEMANTHEMAN
MANTHEMANTHE
ANTHEMANTHEM
THEMANTHEMAN
MANTHEMANTHE
ANTHEMANTHEM
THEMANTHEMAN
MANTHEMANTHE
ANTHEMANTHEM
THEMANTHEMAN
MANTHEMANTHE

AGAINSTAGAINSTAGAINST
TAGAINSTAGAINSTAGAINS
STAGAINSTAGAINSTAGAIN
AGAINSTAGAINSTAGAINST
TAGAINSTAGAINSTAGAINS
STAGAINSTAGAINSTAGAIN
AGAINSTAGAINSTAGAINST
TAGAINSTAGAINSTAGAINS
STAGAINSTAGAINSTAGAIN
AGAINSTAGAINSTAGAINST
TAGAINSTAGAINSTAGAINS
STAGAINSTAGAINSTAGAIN
AGAINSTAGAINSTAGAINST
TAGAINSTAGAINSTAGAINS
STAGAINSTAGAINSTAGAIN
AGAINSTAGAINSTAGAINST
TAGAINSTAGAINSTAGAINS
STAGAINSTAGAINSTAGAIN

GRAPEGRAPEGRAPE
RAPEGRAPEGRAPEG
GRAPEGRAPEGRAPE
RAPEGRAPEGRAPEG
GRAPEGRAPEGRAPE
RAPEGRAPEGRAPEG
GRAPEGRAPEGRAPE
RAPEGRAPEGRAPEG
GRAPEGRAPEGRAPE
RAPEGRAPEGRAPEG
GRAPEGRAPEGRAPE
RAPEGRAPEGRAPEG
GRAPEGRAPEGRAPE
RAPEGRAPEGRAPEG
GRAPEGRAPEGRAPE
RAPEGRAPEGRAPEG

ABANDONEDABANDONED
DABANDONEDABANDONE
ONEDABANDONEDABAND
DONEDABANDONEDABAN
ANDONEDABANDONEDAB
ABANDONEDABANDONED
DABANDONEDABANDONE
ONEDABANDONEDABAND
DONEDABANDONEDABAN
ANDONEDABANDONEDAB
ABANDONEDABANDONED
DABANDONEDABANDONE
ONEDABANDONEDABAND
DONEDABANDONEDABAN
ANDONEDABANDONEDAB
ABANDONEDABANDONED
DABANDONEDABANDONE
ONEDABANDONEDABAND
DONEDABANDONEDABAN
ANDONEDABANDONEDAB

ANTAGONISMANTAGONISM
MANTAGONISMANTAGONIS
ISMANTAGONISMANTAGON
ONISMANTAGONISMANTAG
AGONISMANTAGONISMANT
ANTAGONISMANTAGONISM
MANTAGONISMANTAGONIS
ISMANTAGONISMANTAGON
ONISMANTAGONISMANTAG
AGONISMANTAGONISMANT
ANTAGONISMANTAGONISM
MANTAGONISMANTAGONIS
ISMANTAGONISMANTAGON
ONISMANTAGONISMANTAG
AGONISMANTAGONISMANT
ANTAGONISMANTAGONISM
MANTAGONISMANTAGONIS
ISMANTAGONISMANTAGON
ONISMANTAGONISMANTAG
AGONISMANTAGONISMANT

INHERITINHERIT
ITINHERITINHER
HERITINHERITIN
INHERITINHERIT
ITINHERITINHER
HERITINHERITIN
INHERITINHERIT
ITINHERITINHER
HERITINHERITIN
INHERITINHERIT
ITINHERITINHER
HERITINHERITIN
INHERITINHERIT
ITINHERITINHER
HERITINHERITIN
INHERITINHERIT
ITINHERITINHER
HERITINHERITIN

ARMAMENTARMAMENT
TARMAMENTARMAMEN
MENTARMAMENTARMA
MAMENTARMAMENTAR
ARMAMENTARMAMENT
TARMAMENTARMAMEN
MENTARMAMENTARMA
MAMENTARMAMENTAR
ARMAMENTARMAMENT
TARMAMENTARMAMEN
MENTARMAMENTARMA
MAMENTARMAMENTAR
ARMAMENTARMAMENT
TARMAMENTARMAMEN
MENTARMAMENTARMA
MAMENTARMAMENTAR
ARMAMENTARMAMENT
TARMAMENTARMAMEN
MENTARMAMENTARMA
MAMENTARMAMENTAR

LATERALLATERALLATERAL
ATERALLATERALLATERALL
ALLATERALLATERALLATER
LATERALLATERALLATERAL
ATERALLATERALLATERALL
ALLATERALLATERALLATER
LATERALLATERALLATERAL
ATERALLATERALLATERALL
ALLATERALLATERALLATER
LATERALLATERALLATERAL
ATERALLATERALLATERALL
ALLATERALLATERALLATER
LATERALLATERALLATERAL
ATERALLATERALLATERALL
ALLATERALLATERALLATER
LATERALLATERALLATERAL
ATERALLATERALLATERALL
ALLATERALLATERALLATER
LATERALLATERALLATERAL
ATERALLATERALLATERALL
ALLATERALLATERALLATER

ETHEREALETHEREALETHEREAL
ALETHEREALETHEREALETHERE
REALETHEREALETHEREALETHE
HEREALETHEREALETHEREALET
ETHEREALETHEREALETHEREAL
ETHEREALETHEREALETHEREAL
ALETHEREALETHEREALETHERE
REALETHEREALETHEREALETHE
HEREALETHEREALETHEREALET
ETHEREALETHEREALETHEREAL
ETHEREALETHEREALETHEREAL
ALETHEREALETHEREALETHERE
REALETHEREALETHEREALETHE
HEREALETHEREALETHEREALET
ETHEREALETHEREALETHEREAL
ETHEREALETHEREALETHEREAL
ALETHEREALETHEREALETHERE
REALETHEREALETHEREALETHE
HEREALETHEREALETHEREALET
ETHEREALETHEREALETHEREAL

RICHARD KOSTELANETZ's work has been acknowledged at some length in Ronald S. Berman's *America in the Sixties* (1967), Ihab Hassan's *Contemporary American Literature* (1973), Robert Spiller's *Literary History of the United States* (fourth ed.,1974), *The Reader's Adviser* (1969 & 1974), Daniel Hoffman's *Harvard Guide to Contemporary American Writing* (1979), Irving and Anne D. Weiss's *Thesaurus of Book Digests 1950-1980* (1981), George Myers' *Introduction to Modern Times* (1982), David Cope's *New Directions in Music* (1984), Joan Lyons' *Artists' Books* (1985), Tom Holmes' *Electronic and Experimental Music* (1985), Jamake Highwater's *Shadow Show* (1986), *Columbia Literary History of the United States* (1988), Eric Salzman's *Twentieth-Century Music: An Introduction* (third ed, 1988), Tom Johnson's *The Voice of the New Music* (1989), Robert Siegle's *Suburban Ambush* (1989), John Rodden's *The Politics of Literary Reputation* (1989), *The Reader's Catalog* (1989), Lydia Goehr's *The Imaginary Museum of Musical Works* (1992), *Ecce Kosti* (1996), Bob Grumman's *Of Many Where-at-Once* (1998), Samuel R. Delany's *About Writing* (2005), Kyle Gann's *Music Downtown* (2006), Sally Banes's *Before, Between, and Beyond: Three Decades of Dance Writing* (2007), C. T. Funkhouser's *Prehistoric Digital Poetry* (2007), Jacques Donguy's *Poésies Experimentales Zonenumérique* (1953-2007) (2007), and Geza Perneczky's *Assembling Magazines 1969-2000* (2007), among other critical histories of contemporary culture. Otherwise, he is unrecognized and unclassifiable.

www.ingramcontent.com/pod-product-compliance
Lightning Source LLC
Chambersburg PA
CBHW031139090426
42738CB00008B/1148